Walk in Light and Love

and Love

The Message of First John

Donald L. Alexander

WestBow
PRESS
A DIVISION OF THOMAS NELSON

WestBow Press books may be ordered through booksellers or by contacting:

WestBow Press
A Division of Thomas Nelson
1663 Liberty Drive
Bloomington, IN 47403
www.westbowpress.com
1-(866) 928-1240

ISBN: 978-1-4497-2795-6 (sc)

Library of Congress Control Number: 2011918064

Printed in the United States of America

WestBow Press rev. date: 11/01/2011

Contents

SECTION TWO
The Gospel's Fundamental Ethical Command
"God is Love"(I John 3: 1-5:13)

Dedication/Appreciation

This book is dedicated to two groups. First is to my six grandchildren as they pursue a clearer and deeper understanding of the love and grace of God or seek to grow more mature in their Christian faith. My hope is that this book may make a contribution to their pursuit. The second is to the members of the "Karios adult bible study" who graciously listened and reflectively offered insight into the questions raised and admonitions contained in John's First Epistle. As the Bible study leader, I could not have found a better group of Christians with which to lead a discussion of and address the teachings of First John.

Secondly, I want also to express my appreciation and gratitude to my daughter, Karin, who reformatted the entire manuscript for publication when my computer skills were greatly lacking and to my son, Jonathan, who offered helpful suggestions to an early draft of the book.

Introduction

Gaining a Perspective

GAINING A PERSPECTIVE

Study Questions

Read the section on the introduction (pp. 1-7) and be prepared to discuss the following questions.

(1) What is the view of the salvation presented by the false teachers?

(2) How does John's view of salvation differ from the false teachers?

(3) Cite the three claims concerning sin advocated by the false teachers. (1:6-10)

(4) What is your opinion of Paul Rees' statement on the relationship between the mind and heart?

The writings of the apostle John have long been valued by Christians for their simplicity of language and singularity of purpose. In his Gospel, for example, John presents a distinctive, yet uncomplicated, portrait of Jesus. Jesus is described as "the light of the world;" "the way, the truth, and the life," "the vine," "the good shepherd," and with several distinctive "I am" statements, such as, "I am the bread of life;" and "I am the resurrection and the life."

Singularity of purpose is also evident in John's Gospel. John selects specific sayings and miracles of Jesus with the purpose of confirming the belief that Jesus is the Son of God, the Messiah with the goal of challenging people to believe in Him since only through belief in Christ can people find eternal life. John explicitly writes, *"Jesus did many other miraculous signs in the presence of his disciples which are not recorded in this book But these (specific ones) are written so that you may come to believe that Jesus is the Messiah, the Son of God, and that through believing you may have life in his name*" (John 20:30-31 NRSV).

Three Epistles are also ascribed to the writing of John. The focus of this brief study, however, will center exclusively on John's First Epistle. This Epistle was principally written to resolve arguments and ensuing conflicts within the Johannine community.[1] The conflicts centered over false interpretations of Jesus as the Messiah, ethics, the nature of sin, the last days, and more.[2] The disputes had divided the community into two groups or theological viewpoints. The disagreements had come to an impasse. The result was that some members left the fellowship of the community. John writes, "*They went out from us, but they did not belong to us; for if they had belonged to us, they would have remained with us. But by going out they made it plain that none of them belongs to us*" (2:19-20 NRSV). They left because they were unable to live in a community who proclaimed the truth that Jesus Christ was indeed God come in the flesh.

THE JOHANNINE COMMUNITY

The Johannine community did not constitute in the contemporary sense a congregation or a church. In all likelihood the community was composed of several house churches which together formed the community under the teaching authority of the apostle John. Some scholars, however, have chosen to identify the community as the "Johannine circle." Others selected the identifying phrase, the "Johannine School," recognizing philosophical and religious "schools" that existed during this general period of history. There were, for example, the "schools" of the Pythagoreans, the Stoics, The Essences, of Philo, of Rabbi

Hillel, and - in the Christian era, the Antiochene and Alexandrian schools.[3] These "schools" were characterized by the teacher-pupil relationships and were generally traced to a "founder" who embodied the teaching authority and which, at the same time, determined their independence from comparable so called "schools." [4]

While evidence can be marshaled for the possible existence of a "Johannine school," it seems more appropriate to think of a Johannine "community;" that is, several separate groups of people or house churches that chose to come under the influence and teaching authority of the apostle John. The time of writing cannot be determined with any certainty. Scholarly suggestions range within the time frame of 90-150 C.E., though the mid to late 90's is most probable. The place of writing was likely Ephesus where John has been projected as serving as the Ephesian community's teaching-pastor.[5]

THE UNIQUENESS AND AUTHORSHIP OF FIRST JOHN

John's First Epistle is unique. It is unique because it lacks an opening greeting and a closing benediction. In addition, there is no explicit identification of the author, or a specifically stated audience; such as, "To the churches in Galatia." (Gal. 1:2). While the absence of an identified author is unusual in the New Testament documents, it is not without precedent. (See: The Epistle to the Hebrews). What is unusual, however, is that Second and Third John do name a specific author, identified as the "elder" (presbyteros). Thus the question arises, If Second and Third John were written by the "elder," who, then, wrote First John? The proposed answers are varied, but two seem dominate. On the one hand, some scholars argue that the apostle John and the "elder" of Second and Third John are the same person. In Second and Third John, the apostle simply selects a more "pastoral" title to identify himself in the same manner as Peter did in referring to himself as a "fellow elder" in I Peter 5:1. On the other hand, some, such as, Papias of Hierapolis, an early church writer, and Eusebius, an early historian[6], contend that there were in fact two distinguished church leaders in Asia Minor named "John." But whether John, the beloved disciple, actually penned the First Epistle ascribed to him or it was written by an authorized elder of the church, the content and linguistic style give strong indication that the writer was committed to the apostolic teachings grounded in the Fourth Gospel and that the writer was an eye-witness to the Christ-event. Moreover, the Fourth Gospel and the First Epistle both employ similar key concepts, such as, life (zoe), fellowship (koinonia), truth (aletheia), love (agape), and joy (chara) that lend strong support to identifying the author as the apostle John. At the same time, however, a recognized church leader, schooled under the teaching-leadership of John, might also have penned the Epistle. The weight of evidence, however, points toward the apostle John who served as the teaching-pastor in Ephesus from where the text is proposed to have been written.

This lack of a specifically identified author raises a very important question. Can the inspiration and authority of First John be confirmed by its strong agreement with the "apostolic message" as firmly as if an undisputed credentialed author; say Peter for example, was identified as the writer? In other words, could an authorized leader of the Church write an Epistle in conformity with the Gospel message and simultaneously be regarded as divinely inspired due to the specific content of the letter? A word of caution needs to be voiced here. Is there a tendency in today's Church to be so involved in securing the identity of the author, analyzing the language or specific words of a text that we consequently miss the power of the message? The point is not that the language of the text is unimportant nor the securing of the author's identity meaningless. Rather, language points not to itself but to the reality it describes. If the "reality" is false, the language will not make it true. Does not the message of God's self-revelation have logical priority over the language that proclaims the message? For example, my good friend, Professor Mark Reasoner, is a kind, thoughtful, and dedicated Christian. My language does not make this true. It is true if-and-only-if Mark is indeed kind, thoughtful, and dedicated to Christ. First John has the authority of Scripture, not merely because the beloved disciple John wrote it, but because it proclaims the message of God's redeeming, forgiving, and restoring love exclusively revealed in Jesus Christ.

THE JOHANNINE PROBLEM

The Johannine community was experiencing a theological crisis. Interpretations diametrically opposed to the Gospel message were being advanced. The community was in turmoil, having become divided into two groups. Hostile feelings and unfortunate charges were being made by persons on both sides. The issues needed to be corrected; attitudes needed to be changed; sin needed to be confessed; and unity needed to be restored. Leadership could not hesitate; pastoral action and direction was imperative. Five issues can be discerned that constitute the heart of the disunity. A brief summary of these five issues will provide a helpful background for understanding the concerns and exhortations contained in the Epistle.[7]

Issue One: The Identity and Redemptive Work of Jesus

A major, if not "the" major, issue centered on the question: Who really is Jesus – human or divine, and what precisely did his redemptive work accomplish? The teachers, who opposed the apostolic teaching, re-interpreted the nature of Jesus which at the same time altered the understanding of Jesus' redemptive work.

At the heart of the alternative teaching was the belief that Jesus was not divine. Jesus was an important mediator, but was not on the same level as God. Only the "God of light and goodness" is divine. Since Jesus was a human person, argued the infiltrating teachers, he could not be divine. Being human is incompatible with the attributes of divinity: impassibility, immutability, eternality and perfection. Humans belong to the earthly realm, to the coming to be and passing away that marks all earthy things.

The premise underlying this interpretation was a radical dualism between matter and spirit. The new teachers taught that all matter is evil. Even creation itself, by nature of its material constitution, is evil. The divine, on the other hand, is of the spirit. Only the spirit is good, being free from the contamination of the material. So as long as humans are creaturely, material beings, salvation remains impossible. Salvation, however, can be achieved, but only if the flesh – indeed human existence itself, is transcended. Thus, a new understanding of salvation was proposed. - a salvation that centered exclusively in the "spirit" realm beyond material existence. Being "trapped" in this world, the spiritual dimension of humans yearns to be free from matter and ascend to its true home. John, of course, responds, "This is how you can recognize the Spirit of God: Every spirit that acknowledges that Jesus Christ has come in the flesh is from God, but every spirit that does not acknowledge Jesus is not from God." (4:2b-3a)

Issue Two: The Nature of Salvation

The false teachers taught that something had gone terribly wrong in the world. Humanity's spiritual essence had become radically distorted. This distortion was not the result of something humans had done; such as, Adam's act of disobedience; rather, it was a flaw within the nature of the universe itself. The flaw occurred from the act of creating the visible, physical universe; that is, in the creation of matter which by presupposition is evil.[8]

If salvation, therefore, is to be achieved, it will require transcending our material, fleshly existence by means of special knowledge (gnosis). This knowledge is not knowledge in the ordinary sense; such as, philosophic insight or a correct understanding of the Law, etc. It is spiritual in nature and experience. It entails the recovery of the lost knowledge of what humans once were and were intended to be as spiritual beings. It resides in returning to the life of the spirit, a life free from the evil contamination of the flesh.

This secret knowledge is communicated to us by a (spiritual) "savior" or redeemer who descends from the spirit world above into the world below. This "savior," notes Dodd, "represents a primordial humanity, eternal, unfallen, pre-existent, who descends into the world to redeem its fallen counterpart." (Dodd,1953,p.109f). Given the nature of this "redeemer" figure," a sharp distinction was drawn between the spiritual Christ, who is from above; and the human Jesus who is from below – earthly. This mystical, spirit "redeemer" transmits the special knowledge that renews the mind or spirit. This renewal experience is described as being born again in the mind. In the (Gnostic text) Pistis Sophia, an initiate testifies to being transformed into the divine substance (which is light and spiritual in nature) and so deified. He writes, "I passed into an immortal body, and now I am not what I was before but am born again in nous (mind)."[9]

Issue Three: The Nature of Sin

The false teachers' proclaimed salvation entails the transformation of the mind (nous) or the renewal of the spirit. Once a person achieves this transformation, he is reunited with the Ultimate reality referred to as the Pleroma (Fullness of true existence). Once this state is achieved, sin no longer exists for the initiate. The concept of sin is applicable only to the material things of the world. Since the initiate has been transposed into the spiritual realm above, he no longer commits acts of sin. What occurs in the earthly life cannot affect the newly acquired spiritual state.

Since spiritual transformation entails the special knowledge of one's true home, sin is viewed as ignorance, ignorance of one's true self as part of the ultimate reality or the Pleroma – the true spiritual source of original fullness. To belong to the Pleroma is to exist in a state free from evil or sin. It is to dwell in the perpetual, ineffable "light" of the ultimate God who is "fullness" (Pleroma) and who exists in absolute distinction to the inferior gods who created matter. The "redeemer figure" that is identified with the (spiritual) Christ who specifically came to deliver the special knowledge that transforms the mind and enables believers to be free from the evil conditions of mortal existence. John responds, "If we claim to be without sin, we deceive ourselves and the truth is not in us." (I Jn 1:8).

Issue Four: The Nature of Love

There are no explicit statements within the text of First John that the opposing teachers were immoral in their conduct. They do, however, claim that they are no longer sinners by nature and hence they do not commit acts of sin. They profess to dwell in the "enlightened" state of the spirit beyond the sinful condition of this world. The author of First John, therefore, introduces that thesis that anyone who claims to live in God and God in him must love his brother. His rationale resides in the premise that "God is love."

The Epistle's admonitions about love, however, appear to be directed more to conduct of the children of God than a rebuttal to the false teachers' claims. The author's argument centers on the inherent connection between loving deeds and the knowledge of God. John writes: "Whoever lives in love lives in God and God in him . . . . Whoever does not love does not know God because God is love. . . . This is love, not that we loved God, but that he loved us and sent his Son as an atoning sacrifice for our sins." (I Jn 4:16, 8, 10). Here the agape motif of the New Testament finds its most compelling exposition. We must take great care not only to listen to the author's teaching but also the strength of his message.

Issue Five: The Certainty of Hope

One final issue can be discerned; namely, the hope that distinguishes the children of light from the children of darkness. The author presents several encouraging and admonishing Christian truths with the purpose of assuring the believers of the certainty of their hope in Christ that has become suspect by the doctrinal disputes. First, he points to the great love the Father has lavished on them that constitutes them as the children of God. Second, he argues that the reason for the present conflict is because the world does not know God and simultaneously does not know them. Third, the author informs them that the conflict is evidence that it is the last hour and identifies the false teachers as antichrists. Finally, the author reminds them that they have an "anointing" from Christ so that they do not need to be instructed in the fundamentals truths of the faith by these false teachers. (2:20. 27).

Conclusion: The Central Theme

The message of First John is composed around two key declarations: namely, "God is light" and "God is love." These two statements together convey an important revelation of the nature of God and a critical principle for living the Christian life; namely, that doctrine and lifestyle and truth and practice go hand-in-hand. It might be said that the two constitute a marriage made in heaven. We must take care, therefore, not to over-emphasize one side of the union to the diminishing or neglecting of the other; that is, to love our theological principles more than we love people, especially those who radically disagree with us.

The message of First John stands opposed to a radical dichotomy between the mind and the heart. The union is not simply a harmony between two opposites. Rather, the significance of the opposites makes possible a harmonious unity that is not possible apart from the existence of both sides.

Let me illustrate. Consider the quality of opposition that pertains between a male and a female and of the love relationship created between them. At first the distance of sexual (male and female) identity appears. This difference, however, changes as the two come to enjoy each other's company and a love relationship emerges. A relationship which was first established on a premise of opposition becomes a positive force in the interaction between the two: each increasingly begins to define him/herself in terms of the love relationship. In this relationship the differences are not lost; rather "mutuality heightens individuality." The same is true in the harmonious relationship between belief and practice. A unity is created in which the differences are not removed but united together a powerful witness to the truth of the Gospel emerges that is not present in a single side. The point is that theological beliefs become compelling when expressed in loving ways.

So walk in light and in love. "There is no rift," writes Paul S. Rees, "between the enkindled heart and the enlightened mind. Light without love can be as forbiddingly cold as an iceberg in moonlight. Love without light, on the other hand, can be as flamingly destructive as a forest fire in the dry season. Love as unregulated impulse is dangerous. Love giving itself to hard thinking and sensitive discrimination is a delight to God and a priceless benediction to the Church and society."[10]

Section One

The Gospel's Foundational Claim
"God is Light" (First John 1:1-10)

Lesson One: A Basis for Conduct to be Advocated (1:5)

Study Questions

Read I John 1:1-2:29, note especially 1:5 and pp. 8-17, the reader should be able to:

(1) Interpret the phrase, "God is Light" and explain how its meaning relates to living the Christian life.

(2) Offer an explanation for John's statement that "there is no darkness of any kind" in God. (See: pp. 8-17). Do you agree with the author's viewpoint?

(3) What is your opinion of Ben Witherington's view on evil? Explain!

The arguments and admonitions of First John centers on the declaration that "God is light, and there is no darkness in Him of any kind." But what did John mean by the statement that "God is light"? First, take care not to reverse the declaration and say, "Light is God." If "light" were equivalent with God, we would then find ourselves in the thought world of the false teachers. Light itself is not God, but was created by God. (Gen. 1:3). Contingent things are created things and do not have the source of themselves in themselves; and therefore cannot be equal to God – no matter how fascinating the notion of "light" is. On the other hand, if by "light" is meant to convey the thought that absolute truth and righteousness resides only in God, the answer would be yes.

So we return to the question. What is John's intended meaning by the declaration that "God is light?" A helpful source comes from John's Gospel. According to John's Gospel, the light of God resides in the person and redemptive work of Jesus as the way, the truth, and the life. "In him was life", writes John, "and that life was the light of men. The light shines in the darkness, but the darkness has not understood it." (Jn. 1:4). John again writes, "He (John the Baptist) . . . was not the light; he came only as a witness to the light. The true light that gives light to every man was coming into the world." (Jn. 1:6-8). Later, when informing his disciples of his coming death, Jesus states, "You are going to have the light just a little while longer." He then admonishes them, "Put your trust in the light (the truth revealed in Christ) while you have it, so that you may become sons of light." (John 12:35-36).

It seems correct, then, to interpret John's declaration, "God is light" primarily in a metaphorical sense, but with clear reference to the redemptive and ethical implications that God has come into the world in Jesus Christ. The declaration that "God is Light" is the basis for John's arguments and admonitions in the First Epistle; namely, to confirm belief in Jesus as the Messiah and to encourage Christ-like conduct by walking in the light as he (Jesus) is in the light. John writes, "For whoever claims to live in Christ must walk as Jesus did." (I Jn. 2: 6).

John introduces this fundamental declaration with the statement, "This is the message we heard." (1:5). (The word, "message," used in this grammatical form, occurs only here in New Testament). The word performs an important role for emphasizing the declaration that God is light. Messages have two functions: first to convey information and second to alert the reader or listener with its content. Let me illustrate. In 1945 on a beautiful Sunday afternoon in California, when

I was about five years old, my family was taking a leisurely drive in the country. Suddenly, there was an interruption on the car radio program. With tension evident in his voice, the announcer stated, "President Roosevelt has a special announcement (message) for all Americans," "Pearl Harbor has been attacked by the Japanese and America is at war." I recall my father swearing and mother letting out gasp in unbelief. The message from the President not only informed my parents and all Americans on that day of an important event but also of an event that would impact their lives with uncertainty of the future.

John's declaration furthermore states that "there is no darkness of any kind" in God. In John's Epistle the word "darkness" is used metaphorically to convey the notions of unrighteousness, rejection of the truth, error, evil, sin and hatred (1John 3; 8; 1:9-10). (Later John will identify it with a lack of love: I John 4:8). The point is that persons cannot claim to live in Christ and at the same time to be unconcerned about unrighteousness and sin in their lives. John, therefore, admonishes the members of the community to embrace a serious and disciplined-dedication to the truths and life-style in conformity with the teachings and practices of Jesus. (I John 1: 6). Failure to do so diminishes the truth of the Gospel and our witness to the world.

To claim that there is no darkness of any kind in God has resulted in years of philosophical and theological dialogue. A popular critique has been simplified and formulated into in the following popular argument against the declaration that there is no darkness in God of any kind.

1. If God is all powerful, and;
2. If God is all good, then;
3. Why, then, does evil exists in the world?

The argument is developed as follows: if the Christian claim of the absolute goodness and sovereign power of God is correct, "How, then, could a good and powerful God allow horrific evil to exist in the world?" In other words, if God is indeed all powerful and therefore could stop any act of evil or violence but does not, God, then, cannot be claimed to be good. Or, perhaps, continues the argument, God is not sufficiently powerful to stop evil for evil continues its harmful and destructive ways. [11]

Christian scholars have offered numerous responses to this critique. While many of the Christian responses have failed to be compelling, perhaps a new approach needs to be considered. The need for a different approach has been suggested by N. T Wright in his book, *Evil and the Justice of God*.[12] Professor Wright proposes that we need to reread the Gospels, and reconsider the importance of the atoning work of Christ. Given the complexity of this problem and its long history of academic reflections coupled with the purpose of this book, a detailed academic response is not warranted. Therefore, a few guiding questions will be asked with the goal of engaging the reader in the issue. At the outset, however, a basic principle will be proposed to start the discussion.

A Basic Premise: God is not the source or author of any kind of evil in the world. This premise is a deduction from the declaration that "there is no darkness in God of any kind." James writes, "When tempted, no one should say, God is tempting me. For God cannot be tempted by evil, nor does he tempt anyone, but each is tempted when by his own evil desires, he is dragged away and enticed. But after desire has conceived, it gives birth to sin. (James 1: 13-14)

Question One: What is the original origin of evil?

In the philosophical-religious thought of the West the interpretation was proposed, going back to the early Greek philosophers, that sin finds its source in the limitations of human creatureliness; that is, in human ignorance and finitude.[13] I start our reflections here because of the conviction that Evangelical Christian thought has not developed a positive theology of human creatureliness. Human creatureliness has been denigrated in the Evangelical mind-set having been closely associated with the biblical concept of the "flesh" which by association is connected to the interpretation of the "sinful nature." Consequently, human creatureliness has had no explicit place in the theological agendas of Evangelical doctrine of salvation. Now by "creatureliness" is meant a positive outlook toward humans as biological creatures; that is, those creatures that possess of the breath of life that constitutes a common bond with all creatures that possess the breath of life. [14]

This interpretation has continued in the modern period, though from a different viewpoint, in the writings of Frederick R. Tennant[15] and Frederick Schleiermacher. Tennant, for example, argues that the source of sin lies in our animal nature. It is the result of instincts and patterns of behavior arising from our animal ancestry that continues to persist into the advanced period of the evolutionary process until humans acquire moral consciousness. The evolutionary process, Tennant believed, will eventually produce a dominant sense of moral awareness within humans. With the advancement of this moral-ethical consciousness, our primitive animal instincts would then be controlled and moral-ethical patterns of behavior would prevail.

Frederick Schleiermacher advances essentially the same viewpoint but with the insertion of the component of God-consciousness – the feeling of absolute dependence upon God. While identifying the source of sin with the Pauline concept of the "flesh" which he interprets as "the totality of the so-called lower powers of the soul," he contrast the "flesh" with his concept of the "spirit" which denotes humanity's "higher" or moral propensities that emerge with God-consciousness. It is in the conflict between the lower and higher powers of human experience that sin occurs. In essence, sin is the result of the powerful desires and passion of physical existence in the absence or incapacity of the spirit. – the higher moral powers awaken by an awareness of God.

One difficulty encountered by the position that human creatureliness is the primary source of sinful acts lies in its inability to account adequately for the diversity of human evil. The evil perpetuated by humans is far too complex and extensive in its expression to be limited to human creatureliness. From the sin of Cain to the modern cruelty and violence initiated, for example, by such persons a Adolf Hitler, Pol Pot, or Malosevic, to say nothing of the greed and desire for status and power evident in structural evil, indicates that a creaturely basis for sin does not provide a sufficient answer. Nor does it appear to be the case that the evolutionary process has lessened in any significant way the enormity and frequent pointlessness of human misdeeds. Something more than creatureliness is at work.

From a Christian viewpoint, a second difficulty centers in the fact that natural desires are not in themselves sinful; at least not in the original purposes of God. The desires of human creatureliness were created by God for the benefit and pleasure of humans. If this is the case, is it not reasonable to conclude that natural desires have come under the control of other forces – forces that pervert them toward improper thinking and acting, resulting in various selfish and inhumane acts? Moreover, since human violence continues unabated to the present, is it not legitimate to ask how much longer must humanity linger in the evolutionary-development process for this higher level of moral awareness to alter human conduct in a significant way?" Something other than creatureliness seems to be at work, conscripting creaturely capacities for its evil purposes.

Finally, it seems logical to hold the view that moral responsibility does not naturally arise from within creatureliness but is imposed upon creaturely existence by means of some external criterion, such as, God, the value of human life, the necessity of civil order, natural law, etc. Contrary to Kant's insistences that morality must be autonomous, I would agree with John Smith, "that no view of the moral life, no serious doctrine of what humans ought to do, can be sustained apart from some transcendent reference to which it is itself subject and judged." [16]

Accepting momentarily that evil does not find its source or origin in God, the biblical teaching states that the original origin of evil resides in the rebellion of Satan against God's authority, power, and position. Believing himself to be equal to God in power, authority, and position, Satan sought to displace God and to place himself at the center of divinity as the absolute sovereign over God's good creation. Ignoring the fact that he was indeed a creature created by God's grace, and that he did not possess the power he claimed to have, only divine judgment awaits his ill-conceived plan. The divine judgment for Satan and his companions was to be cast out of heaven and hurled to earth where they promote evil and perversions of all kinds. Scripture, therefore, identifies Satan as "the god of this age," meaning the god of this present world. (II Cor. 4: 4). In the Book of Revelation, John writes, "The great dragon was hurled down – that ancient serpent called the devil or Satan who leads the whole world astray. He was hurled to the earth and his angels with him" (Rev. 12:9). Identifying Satan "as the god of this age" does not entail that every act of evil that occurs in the world is the direct result of Satanic activity or involvement.

Question Two: What, if any, is the purpose of the continued existence of evil in the world?

In the original temptation recorded in Holy Scripture (Read: Gen. 3: 1-8), Satan's purpose was not only to displace God from God's position as God but also to corrupt and to destroy the relationship between God and the creature created in God's image. The original approach did not principally center on the temptation to disobey God's command, "not to eat," but to sever the trust or faith relationship between them. The goal was to create a heart of disbelief in the goodness of God. The aim was to create distrust in the goodness and loving character of God and God's Word, a distrust that God must overcome to restore the faith relationship again.

Question Three: What is Satan's approach in tempting us to sin and abandon belief in the loving-goodness of God?

According to the Genesis account, the tempter enters the arena and engages Eve in serious discussion about the goodness of God and by implication the true meaning of human existence. The discussion carries strong religious overtones. The Tempter does not come as a wild-eyed monster with a fiery-red face. He comes as an advocate of God, as a supposed member of the household of faith. He does not say, "Come, I will teach you how to sin." Rather, he comes as a sympathetic friend, an understanding colleague, and as a defender of the good. He enters the arena as a comrade, as one who is genuinely concerned. He projects the finest the world has to offer and the best that could be given for our happiness and pleasure. His method, however, is that of concealment, a hiding of his true intent. Sin, therefore, comes in enticing and disguised ways. It masquerades as the good. It boasts itself to be religious, meeting, as nothing else can, our deepest and most personal needs. It promises to open our eyes and to make us like God, enabling us to be the sovereign master and controller of our lives and future destiny.

The goal of the tempter – then, as now, is to interject doubt and mistrust in the Word of God, and thus to destroy the faith-relationship. The words of the Evil One are carefully chosen, "Did God really say?" (Gen 3:1). His approach is skillfully formulated, "Do not misunderstand," he clarifies, "I do not want you to start doubting God. Just the opposite! I want you simply to think about it. God is deceiving you, implies the tempter, God knows that the day you eat you will be "like God knowing good and evil". For this reason, God hides the truth from you.

Question Four: What has God done to break the power of sin and evil in the world?

Like the original rebellion of Satan against God, Satan and his companions continue to foolishly believe that they will ultimately triumph over God; that evil will in the end discredit and thereby defeat belief in the loving goodness of God. But as the apostle Paul writes, "God made you alive with Christ. He forgave us all our sins, having cancelled the written code with its regulations, that was against us, and that stood opposed to us; He took it away, nailing it to the cross. And having disarmed the powers and authorities, He made a public spectacle of them, triumphing over them by the cross." (Col. 2: 13-15). The goal of Satan and his cohorts is to cause believers to doubt God's love and goodness and attempt to prove that evil is stronger than God.

Question Five: While evil, suffering, and the sin continues to exist in our world, what can believers realistically expect from God?

NT. Wright proposes that a re-examination of the gospels and the atoning work of Jesus may give us a better approach to the problem of evil than the traditional philosophical ones. A re-reading of the Gospels may offer a more satisfying response to the suffering and evil, especially for suffering and pain experienced by believers in view of the promises of God. Recognizing that the biblical message takes the problem of evil and suffering with great seriousness and that evil and suffering are not merely the consequence of some failure in the evolutionary process or psychological dysfunctions of creaturely existence, consider the following question asked by John Claypool: "What can believers like us honestly expect of God in the daily struggles and sufferings of life in this world? If those promises mean that God somehow comes to our rescue, becoming a part of our human life, what exactly can or should we expect from God?" [17](p.38) Claypool suggests that there is not one answer but three.

The first answer is a miracle. Of course, a miracle is our first choice. A miracle brings immediate healing and abolishes our pain and suffering. Augustine defined a miracle as "God choosing to do quickly what God usually does at a more deliberate pace."[18] Claypool remarks, "To be open to the miraculous is simply to be true to the data of history. It means not concluding, on the basis of certain assumptions that things cannot happen, when in fact we finite creatures have no sense of what is possible in so vast a realm of mystery." [19]

The second answer is called a "pattern of collaboration." Claypool suggests that some times when God comes to us in troubled times, he offers to do something with us. Claypool clarifies, "I am suggesting that when the divine presence inspires us to be creative and ingenious, God invites us to do something toward the solution of our problem. The collaboration form of God's coming is just as valid as the miraculous." [20] An example of collaboration is God's calling Moses in the setting of his people free. From the experience of the burning bush, God spoke to Moses, "I want you to go and collaborate with me in setting my people free" Often when God speaks to us in this way, we back off. We prefer a miracle. Collaboration, it seems to me, would include God's grace in the skill of doctors and the development of medicines and medical technologies that cure many of our illnesses. Claypool writes, "The point I'm trying to make is that many of the problems for which we very much need divine help are going to be solved when we yoke ourselves to the energies of God; instead of asking God to do everything for us." [21]

The final answer is the one I have personally found helpful in dealing with the problem of suffering and evil: namely, that God comes to be "with us," and remains beside us. God breaks in from beyond and does something for us. Claypool again writes, "There are some times that the help that God offers us is simply the power to endure what cannot be changed, to allow the change to take place within us and our attitude rather than in the outward circumstances that we face." [22] The testimony of many Christians who have experienced suffering that would result in their death bear witness that in times of despair they found a nearness of Christ that produced an inexplicable peace, hope, and confidence that helped them to endure and to overcome fear and the power of death. To believe in God's love, writes Claypool "is to believe that love conquers all, and that the God of love is always by your side. It is to believe that whatever happens, you are not alone – you are in God's hands and these hands are loving hands."[23] The testimony of a Christian diagnosed with incurable cancer was that he would not change his experience with cancer because of an extra-ordinary experience of God's loving presence that he had during his time of suffering and uncertainty.

I find this approach to the problem of suffering and evil personally compelling. No matter how much we suffer, God is beside us and his loving presence sustains us. This is the very love and approach that not only explains the suffering of the cross but also the very depths of God's love for us. God with us is the great mystery. God will never abandon us, but gives us the certainty of hope. Hope is to have confidence that whatever happens, we are in God's hands, and that these hands are loving hands.[24] Preaching at the death of his son Eric, David Bartlett expresses his confidence in the loving care of God. He writes, "I am persuaded that God's love for Erik is stronger than death's power. I am persuaded that the (suffering and) death of Jesus Christ (on the Cross) and the resurrection of Jesus Christ in light and love are not just ancient tradition but present hope – for us, for Erik, for all those we love".[25]

I can personally bear witness to the experience of God's coming to be with us in a time of suffering and in the uncertainty of the physical outcome. I had the unfortunate experience of having what is called a "bleeding on the brain." A blood vessel in my head began to leak and the blood needed to be removed by surgery. In addition, while in the hospital,

I contracted pneumonia and nearly died from the illness. The month long recovery process, however, was slow and often discouraging. During a particular time of depression from the uncertainty, sensing that I may never again preach or teach, coupled with the concern about assisting in my grandchildren's growing faith, I was in prayer and suddenly I sensed an unusual presence of God that reassured me that whatever would happen, I was in his loving and caring hands. In my 50 years of preaching and teaching the gospel, I had never had such an overwhelming sense of God's presence that made me aware in an extra-ordinary way that death was merely a door and not a threat to the fullness of life. The power of suffering resides in fear of death and for persons outside of Christ the fear of the unknown. The Bible makes it explicitly clear that we are not immune to suffering and pain. John writing in the Book of Revelation conveys the message of Jesus to the churches to endure in the face of suffering in the context of what Christ has done for them. The incentive to endure has its focus on the eternal future that God has promised. John writes, "Now the dwelling of God is with men, and he will live with them. They will be his people and God himself will be their God. He will wipe every tear from their eyes. There will be no more death or mourning or crying or pain, for the old order of things has passed away." (Rev. 21: 3b-4)

Ben Witterington III in commenting of John's view of radical evil, writes, "It seems that much of the way John views government and God's solution to the human dilemma is grounded in his belief that evil has a radical hold on the world, including the world of human beings. Because of the evil in creation, judgment is coming. Because evil is so deep-seated and radical, it cannot be dealt with by a this-worldly judgment. Rather judgment takes the form of the end of the world. God wipes the slate clean. He will not allow evil to have immortality, so He brings the whole historical process to an end. The human solution to evil is so fraught with evil that the very solution to evil itself breeds evil. Here evil is a mystery that only God can ultimately resolve. In such a frame of reference, prayer seems like the most important thing the people of God can do for the world. Evil is rampant; God needs to act; do pray"[26] and I would add, trust God even when things are tough going.

LESSON TWO: ERRORS IN CONDUCT TO BE AVOIDED (1:6-10)

Study Questions

Re-read this section (1:6-10) and (note also: pp. 16-17), how would you answer the following questions:

(1) Cite the specific errors that the false teachers claim for themselves. (See 1:6-10)

(2) Give a personal definition of the nature of sin.

(3) In what specific ways do sinful acts affect our relationship with God and our personal charter? (Note verses 1:6,8,10).

The apostle John addresses the threefold claim of the false teacher concerning the nature and practice of sin. The claims are as follows:

(1) The denial that sin breaks fellowship with God (1:6-7).
(2) The denial that sin exists within human nature (1:8-9).
(3) The denial that sin shows itself in our conduct (1:10).

The belief of the false teacher resided in the conviction that sin is the result of human creatureliness; that is, it is due to having physical bodies or material existence. They argued that if one is sufficiently in the Spirit, one does not sin. John, on the other hand, teaches that sin breaks fellowship with God.

But what precisely do we mean by sin? On the one hand, it must be distinguished from civil disobedience. While civil disobedience is not in itself sinful, it can become sinful. For example, if I am driving my car and I am traveling at 70 miles per hour while the speed limit is 40 miles per hour, I am breaking civil law, but I am not technically sinning. Sin always involves relationship with God. Five of the dominant definitions of sin adopted within the various Evangelical denominations are:

(1) Sin is a lack of conformity to the moral law of God, either purposefully or accidentally. (Reformed View)

(2) Sin is a voluntary (purposeful or deliberate) transgression of God's known law. (Wesleyan View)

(3) Sin is essentially the choice of self as the supreme end which constitutes the antithesis of supreme love to God; it is selfishness. (Reinhold Neibuhr's view)

(4) Sin is a failure to love God and neighbor as God has commanded. (Roman Catholic)

(5) Sin is a deliberate blocking of the relational core of human existence . . It is the structural de-creation – the structural remaking of the world. (Mary Grey)

At this point in the text we encounter a serious conflict between John and the false teachers.[27] The conflict centers in claim by the false teachers that they have communion with God and simultaneously are sinless (1:8) while their unethical way of life does not correspond to the claim that God is light.[28] The point of John's exhortation is that we cannot claim to know God and engage in a lifestyle contrary to that claim. The claim at the heart of the conflict is that they have fellowship with God. Christian behavior cannot be separated from Christian experience nor can the Christian ethical-moral lifestyle be divorced from the Christian teachings and value system inherent in the faith.

As believers, committed to the Lordship and teachings of Jesus Christ, we must beware of hypocrisy. The lostness and confusion of our world needs a living interpretation of the Gospel in the lives of those who profess to be Christ's disciples. Persons hungering and searching for the truth need more than abstract, rational arguments. They need to see that the Christ-life is, at the same time, human life – life in its integrated wholeness. When we live in sin, and simultaneously pretend to be Christ's disciples, we not only nullify the truth of the Gospel but we also transform the truth into insignificance.

LESSON THREE: AN ENCOURAGEMENT IN CONDUCT TO BE ANTICIPATED (2:1-8)

Study Questions

Read I John 2:1-3 and pp. 18-19, and be prepared to discuss the following questions:

(1) What is the basis upon which God can grant
     forgiveness of sin?

(2) Explain the meaning of the word; "Advocate"
     (2:1).

(3) What is the significance of Jesus as a "sacrifice of
     atonement? (2:2)

(4) How do you explain in verse 2:2 that Jesus is a
     "sacrifice of atonement" for sin, not only for ours,
     "but also for the whole world?"

(5) Do you agree with the author's explanation that
     there is an indispensible and harmonious connec-
     tion between the work of Christ and the work of
     the Holy Spirit? (Read pp.18-19)

God's judgment upon sin is overwhelmed by God's
grace. This unprecedented manifestation of grace finds its
source in the very nature of God, concretely expressed in
God's Word of promise. The promise of God comes forth as
a Word of hope, of rescue, of redemption, of love, and of life
itself. Upon the occasion of the first sin, there is immediately
issued the promise of a "Redeemer," (Gen. 315), described
as Immanuel, "God with us (Isa. 7:14) and identified as
the "Mighty God" (Isa 9:6). Out of the graciousness and
love of God's nature the promise comes forth: a promise
of reconciliation, of forgiveness (Ezek. 36:24-25), and the
possession of a new heart and a new spirit. (Ezek. 36:26).

John, however, is a realist. He acknowledges that sin
may indeed have occurred and, therefore, in the light of
the triumph of Christ over the power of sin, he urges them
not to sin. Sin has the stench of death about it. Why would
anyone want to risk freedom in Christ for the momentary

pleasure of sin? Sin robs our confidence in Christ, diminishes our freedom, and fills us with guilt. Strecker notes that the clause "in order that you may not sin" (2:1) refers back to 1:5-10. In 1:5-10 the possibility of distancing oneself from sin is presented and given its foundation. (p. 35-36). However, being a realist, John anticipates the possibility of sin in the congregation ("If anyone does sin" 2:1b) and points them to the one who is the foundation of divine forgiveness; namely, Jesus Christ, the Righteous One, corresponding to 1:9. Jesus himself is the representative of God's righteousness as the "Righteous One who is our advocate or defender. . . . "As the representative and revealer of God's righteousness, the sphere of holiness and sinlessness, he places on the community the obligation to be "righteous" in conduct, as Christ is righteous. The community depends on such mediation because it is aware of unrighteousness within its own ranks. If sin is indeed present within the community, the situation should not be denied or overlooked. Nevertheless, the issue should not cause the community to despair or to surrender its hope; rather, the community is to confess and call on Jesus Christ as the Paraclete – our Defender before God.

The use of the word Paraclete is critical to John's message. It is unique in that it only appears in this grammatical form in First John and is applied to Jesus Christ as our advocate. (Other grammatical forms are found in the Fourth Gospel and are applied to the work of the Holy Spirit.) (Jn 14:16, 26; 16:17; 15: 26). It is important to observe that John introduces here an inseparable connection between the redemptive work of Jesus and the work of the Holy Spirit. George Hendry put it this way, "The New Testament knows no work of the Spirit except in and through the work of the Christ."[29] N. Q Hamilton draws the same conclusion, "The Spirit so effectively performs His office of communicating to believers the benefits of the risen Christ that for all intents and purposes the Lord Himself is present bestowing grace on His own.[30]

While the word, Paraclete, has been variously translated as "helper" and "advisor," in all likelihood, the better translation is that of "advocate," that is, Christ is the One who on the basis of his life and redemptive work defends (as our advocate) us before the Father and who has given us the right to be called the "children of God." (3:1). The term, however, is generally used in legal contexts; that is, contexts where judgment is in focus as in 2:1 where the Father's judgment is in view and John 16: 8-11 where the Holy Spirit will judge the world with regard to sin and righteousness. The basis upon which Jesus is declared our "advocate" (parakleton) is that He is also our sacrifice of atonement (hilasmos) before the bar of divine judgment.

John uses the word hilasmos (translated as "atoning sacrifice") again in 4:10: "he loved us and sent his son as an "atoning sacrifice for our sins." Interestingly, John broadens the application. Christ's atoning sacrifice is not for us only but also for the whole world. (2:2). God's vision of redemption focuses on the entire world. Here is a basis for world evangelism. While God hates sin since sin destroys God's purpose in creating the world, God, nevertheless, loves sinners and sent his Son that they also may find life in Him.

LESSON FOUR: AN EXAMPLE IN CONDUCT TO BE AFFIRMED 2:3-8

Study Questions

Read I John 2:3-8 and discuss the following questions:

(1) What in your view is the relationship between the knowledge of God and loving God?

(2) What is the new commandment to which John refers?

(3) Explain the relationship between the knowledge and lifestyle or between doctrine and practice.

(4) Is Paul Rees' view on the relationship between the mind and the heart helpful here. (p.7)? Explain your thoughts!

(5) Do you agree or disagree with the author's statement that the focus on the commandment is not on legal conformity to the law but rather stresses "trust" or "faith" in Christ?

Stephen Smalley contends that there is a definite link between this section and the previous one. The connecting cord is the nature of Christian belief and practice. True Christians are called to reject sin and to develop a loving disposition toward others. Developing a loving disposition by God's grace and the ministry of the Holy Spirit also entails obedience to God's commands. The guiding example for this admonition is the life and conduct of Jesus. (2:3).

Jesus is the true light that has come into the world. In his Gospel John clearly write, "In him (Jesus) was life, and that life was the light of men. The light shines in the darkness, but the darkness has not understood it."(John 1:4) In his Epistle, John reaffirms this truth, "I am writing you a new command, its truth is seen in him (Jesus) and the true light is already shining." John, then, restates the negative side: "Anyone who claims to be in the light, but hates his brother is still in the darkness" (2:4) But "Whoever loves his brother lives in the light and there is nothing in him to make him stumble." Strecker captures John's thought when he writes, "One who hates a brother is like a blind person who cannot find his or her way".[31] John's intention here is to challenge the community to avoid sinful conduct. His admonition centers on the demand not to engage in hatred, but to create within themselves a loving, Christ-like disposition.

Love not only constitutes the core essence of God's nature, but is also the key criterion for defining the child of God. John, therefore, exhort the believers on the necessity of obedience to the command to embrace the light and to walk in love. Smalley expresses it this way, "To have fellowship with God, we must not only acknowledge what the light reveals as true; we must realize in action what it reveals as right."[32]

The relationship here between light and love is not intended to be a theological one; that is, the relationship between knowing God and human action; that is, "John is not interested at this point," notes Georg Strecker, "in making a systematic theological statement."[3] Rather, "The question of the criterion for knowing God aims at practical spiritual counsel;" that is, to keep the command to love our brothers and sister and not to sin. To claim that we are walking in the light while hating our brother, such a person states John, is not only self-deceived about his or her relationship with God, but is also living a lie.

Two observations need to be made at this point. First, John's exhortations to ethical behavior; namely to obey the command to love, are grounded in an awareness of the atoning and forgiving event of Christ' as our "advocate" and as a "sacrifice of atonement" for our sins. (2:1-2). Second, the exhortation to obedience is not presented in legal terms but entails the fact that obedience is first and foremost an act of "trust" and love." An act of disobedience in essence constitutes a sin because it entails choosing our own way and the rejection of God's guiding and protecting Word. That obedience is not presented in a legal manner is supported by the John's use of the word, "command" and not the word, "Law." Furthermore, in 2:3 John writes, If we obey his commands" while later in 2:5 he expresses the same idea with the phrase, "if anyone obeys his word." Georg Strecker insightfully comments, "The injunction to keep God's commandment is not exhausted within the sphere of ethics, but remains open to the eschatological (redemptive) claim that although it includes the ethical commandments, demands still more: it requires faith in the sending of the Son (5:4-5) and rest on the 'word of life.'"[34]

A pastoral note: If a believer establishes a relationship with God as legal based relationship as a means of remaining in the love and grace of God, his or her life will end up either in hypocrisy or despair. The law is never positive in a sin-erupting situation. No matter how determined or disciplined a person may be, any failure in a legal based relationship will intensify the sin failure issuing in despair.

Let me illustrate: Suppose for sake of discussion that the single, most fundamental spiritual requirement for achieving and demonstrating a godly life is closing your eyes every time you pray. Suppose further that you are exceptionally faithful in this task; that is during the past fifteen years you have never failed to close your eyes at the time of prayer. Consequently, you are regarded as a pillar of godliness among your Christian friends and a candidate for "eldership" in the church.

One day, however, as the time of prayer arrived, you closed your eyes as was your disciplined godly practice. But, suddenly and unexpectedly, a strange noise erupts and you instinctively opened your eyes - a clear violation of your standard for maintaining your relationship with God. At that moment, however, the law springs into action. "You opened our eyes and you are, therefore, guilty of breaking the law   the prescribed standard of godliness," is the law's condemning accusation. But you protest: "It was only a peek!" Beside, this is the first and only violation in fifteen years." But the law is not interested in good excuses." You opened your eyes and are clearly guilty of breaking the law, is the indisputable judgment of the law. "You are no longer worthy to be regarded as a godly person," is the law's accusation. Thus, in a sin-activated situation, the purpose of the law is not to affirm our many good deeds but to intensify our sin-failure and to count us as unworthy to be the child of God.

John, encouragingly, is focusing on the positive side of obedience. When believers love as God commands, they are "complete" (without offense) since agape love places complete love and trust in God's commands. Later, John writes, "Whoever lives in love lives in God, and God in him. In this way love is made fully manifest (complete) among us. There is no fear in love. But perfect love drives out fear, because fear has to do with punishment.' (4:16-17). A loving disposition, therefore, cannot be created by simply adhering to a predetermined set of standards, no matter how religious or pious they are. A Loving-disposition is formed when we allow the truth of God's Word to take root in our minds and hearts so that the Holy Spirit, then, can produce in us those virtues that mark us as followers of Christ. John, therefore, I wish to argue, is not making a systematic theological statement about loving one's brothers and sisters, but is giving spiritual counsel. His underlying premise resides in the encouraging and sustaining teaching of 2:1-2; namely, that "the atoning, forgiving, and transforming event of salvation in Christ accompanies every phase of (his) ethical admonitions."[35]

LESSON FIVE: EVIDENCES IN CONDUCT TO BE ADVANCED (2: 9-17)

Test One: Ethical test: Love your neighbor (2: 9-14)

Study Questions

(1) What is the "new commandment to which John refers, though it is not completely new?

(2) Do you agree or disagree with the author's statement that the focus of the commandment is not on legal conformity to the law but stresses "trust" in Christ?

(3) Does the admonition to "obedience" primarily point to an act of trust more than simply fulfilling a required task?

(4) How do you interpret the threefold classification of the community of believers in 2:12-14?

John now turns the attention of the believers to the positive command that they have known from the past, but now has new force and evidence in the life of Jesus Christ; namely, to love their brothers. Evidence of the knowledge of God is manifest in the love of one's brothers and sisters. John writes, "Whoever loves his brother lives in the light, and there is nothing in him to make him offensive." (2:10). Of course, the opposite is equally true; the one who "hates" his brother, writes John, "lives in the darkness and walks in the darkness; he does not know where he is going, because the darkness has blinded him." (2: 11).

Later in 3:5 John will substitute the term "logos" for commandment. This substitution is meaningful. It implies that keeping the commandments is more than a religious obligation; in other words, the keeping of the commandment, as Strecker observes, "is not exhausted within the sphere of ethics, but remains open to the eschatological claim that, although it includes the ethical commandment, demands still more: it required faith in God's Son (cf. 5: 4-5) and rests on the word of life in which the love of God has reached its goal" in the promised redemption.[36] John expressed it this way, "But if anyone obeys this word, God's love is truly made complete or perfect in him." (2:5) John employs the word, (teleiousthai), translated as "complete" (NIV) or perfect (RSV). The verb is used in classical Greek to mean "to bring to an end or fulfillment, or to bring to its goal/ accomplishment,' carrying also a personal sense of bringing to "maturity."[37] The point is that the believer who knows how to love not only knows God but also reflects the character of God because, as John will later discuss, "God is love."

Additional evidences in Christian conduct cited by John comes in three categories in 2:12-14; namely, children, young men, and fathers. The precise meaning of John in employing these three categories, given the context, remains somewhat uncertain. However, two possible options are evident. First, the categories can be interpreted "literally," thereby suggesting actual age groups within the Johannine community. However, the attending descriptions of each category seem to contradict this approach. Second, the categories can be interpreted metaphorically. They are intended to describe levels of spiritual experience and understanding within the community. This viewpoint harmonizes better with the accompanying descriptions. This approach would then interpret "children" as denoting those persons within the community who are new or young in the faith, having recently come to faith. "Young Men" would then seem to convey a group of persons in the community who have fought a good fight against temptation and the adversaries of the faith. "Fathers," then, describes those who are mature in the faith, having believed from the "beginning," that is, on first encounter with the gospel message and have remained faithful.

Test Two: Cosmological Test: "Love not the world" (I John 2: 15-17)

Study Questions

(1) What is your interpretation of John's use of the word "world" in the admonition, "Do not love the world."?

(2) Can you offer an explanation for the three individual descriptions of the "world" offered by John in 2:16?

(3) Offer an explanation that the two statements of John: "God so loved the world" and "Do not love the world" are not contradictory?

The object of the imperative in 2:15-17 is the "world." By the term, "world," John does not mean the physical universe. John's concern here is ethical, not physical. There is, however, no contradiction in John's admonitions here between "God so loved the world," and the command "not to love the world." An ethical context removes any proposed contradiction. The point John is making is that the "world" denotes an orientation, a lifestyle under the control of evil and self centered ways contrary to the command to love one's neighbor, and that is opposed to the will and ways of God. Strecker put it this way, "The worldly way of being excludes communion with the Father (2·15) This is especially apparent in human beings' unethical behavior. Anyone who lives "in the world" (en w kosmw) and is, at the same time, of the world (ek tou kosmou) is ruled by that which belongs to the world; namely, its pleasures and passions. (epithymia).[38]

John then proceeds to delineate more specifically what constitutes "being of" or "living by" the world. It is to be dominated by physical urges (the lust of the flesh), or to be controlled by the desires initiated by the visual stimuli (the lust of the eyes), or by the "pride of riches." The word alazoneia, translated as the pride of life conveys more than simply the pride or arrogance that riches can produce. John describes these as the things that belong to the world; namely, the love of status or position over the care and concern of others. (2:16). To love these things diminishes or excludes the love of the Father. While we are "in" the world, we do not belong to the world. To love the world and the things of the world is to have embraced a disposition, as Stephen Smalley expressed it, which is "anchored to a society which by nature does not know God, and is inclined to reject him."[39] These worldly attributes have been contemporized this way: (1) The lust of the flesh – as sensuality in character; (2) The lust of the eyes – as superficiality in character; (3) The pride of life – as pretentiousness in attitude. I personally interpret the phrase, "the pride of life" as pretending to be more in status or position than one actually is or the desire to impress others by one's possession or status. In this command "not to love the world," John is not proposing a philosophical thesis, instead, "this is a conclusion drawn from empirical experience that worldly existence is ephemeral;"[40] that is, transitory or passing away.

Test Three: Theological Test "God has come in the flesh" (2:18-27)

Study Questions

(1) Can you explain John's use of plural form of the term, "antichrist"?

(2) What constitutes the precise error that causes John to refer to the false teachers as "antichrists'?

(3) What is John's meaning of the phrase, "last hour"?

John now turns his attention (2: 18-27) directly to the false teaching. Verse 2:18, therefore, introduces a new topic. Spiritual admonitions are dropped and clear theological instructions and challenges are presented. John is speaking directly now to the Christian community. Three clear emphases can be deduced from this section. (1) The first theological point occurs in 2:18-21. The focus is eschatological; namely, "it is the last hour." (2:18). The sentence, "it is the last hour" is firmly grounded in the early Christian tradition, going back to the oldest patristic tradition in Polycarp.[41] The future time has arrived, and John's rationale for his conviction is that many antichrists have come. This view is identical to that stated in Second John verse 7. The Presbyter writes, "Many deceivers, who do not acknowledge Jesus Christ has come in the flesh, have gone out into the world and are described as deceivers and antichrists." That antichrists will come is known by the Johannine community, as the phrase, "as you have heard" verifies. (2:18). Anthony Hoekema writes that the signs of the coming of the Lord to which believers are knowledgeable were: (1) tribulations (2) apostasy, and (3) the presence of antichrist.[42] The coming of the Lord is at hand for John. While the community has experienced tribulations and apostasy, it is the presence of the false teachers whom he identifies as antichrists that prompts John's declaration that "it is the last hour." Georg Strecker writes, "The community's own story is being played out in the immediate context of the apocalyptic events of the end times." [43]

What precisely does John mean by identifying the false teachers as "antichrists"? Despite the discussions and disagreements of believers about who "the" antichrist is and his role in the end times, the word, "antichrist," appears in the New Testament only in the Epistles of John. (twice in 2:18; and once in 2:22; 4:3; 2Jn 1:7). Moreover, John uses the word in the plural rather than the singular, implying that the term does not refer to a distinct individual but more specifically to a belief system that embodies a persistent rejection of Christ; or even more specifically, of persons who deny that Jesus Christ has come in the flesh and whose conduct and outlook is in opposition to God's Word, particularly in its teaching that Jesus is not divine but only a human person. Strecker notes that "antichrist" is "clearly distinguished from the power from which the antichrist comes and to which he belongs."[44] It is, nevertheless, the presence of antichrists that constitutes the criterion by which the believers may recognize that the end time has arrived and may prepare themselves for the end. The pervasive presence of evil, particularly the presence of teachers who deny that Jesus is indeed God Himself come into human existence for the redemption of humankind, embodies the outlook of the antichrists.

An Apostate Teaching to be Denounced (2: 22-23)

Study Questions

(1) What constitutes for John the primary error of the false teachers?

(2) Explain why a fundamental confession of the Gospel centers on the humanity of Jesus?

(3) Explain the theological significance of the humanity of Christ or the incarnation as essential for the redemption of humankind?

John urges his followers to keep the faith. The false teachers are challenging the core of their faith-confession with the insistence that Jesus is not God. Since Jesus has a human body, he cannot, therefore, be divine. To embrace such a belief is to reject an essential confession of the Christian faith. We must never diminish or alter this central confession. Without it, we empty the redemptive message of the promise of forgiveness of sin and newness of life. The false teachers have rejected the application of the title "Christ" to Jesus which also entails denying to Jesus the privilege of being God's Son (5:5-6). For John, as well as for Christians today, "there is no such thing as faith in God apart from the historical revelation of God in Jesus."[45] Apart from the incarnation God's love and redemptive purpose is unknowable. John therefore explicitly declares, "To confess the Son is to have the Father, that is, to know and acknowledge the Father. (See: 2:3, 4, 5, 14).

Second John 9, the teaching of the false teachers has created uncertainty and confusion about this core truth of the faith. While not directly stated, it appears that the false teachers claim to have had a special "anointing" (charisma = special spiritual knowledge) by which they deny the confessional statement that "Jesus is the Christ and the Messiah" in order to confirm and to convince members of the congregation that their belief concerning Jesus is correct.

John, therefore, responds, "See that what you have heard from the beginning remains in you. . . . As for you, the anointing (the truth about the deity of Christ as the Son of God (See: Fourth Gospel 20:31) remains in you, you (therefore) do not need anyone (such as, the false teachers) to teach you." (2:24,27). John's use of the word, charisma/anointing in this context, does not primarily refer to an anointing of the Holy Spirit, though the work of the Holy Spirit is certainly involved, but to the truth of the Gospel message about Jesus which the Holy Spirit confirms in the heart of the believer. This truth about Jesus as the Son of God is what the community learned and heard from the beginning. (2:27). John urges them to keep this core "truth" alive in their hearts and minds. The word "to abide" or "remain" carries the idea of "to endure" or "to persist."[46] The text implies that the believers should persist in the teaching of Christ. "Anyone who runs ahead or does not continue in the teachings of Christ," writes John, does not have God; whoever continues in the teaching has both the Father and the Son." (v:9).

John counters the claim of the false teachers that they alone possess the correct spiritual truth because of their special anointing with the assertion that the believers do not possess the truth. John writes, "I do not write to you because you do not know the truth, but because you do know it." (2:21).The truth is that God Himself has come in the person of Jesus Christ as the Son of God. Anyone who denies this truth, bluntly states John, is a liar (2:22) By "liar" John means he does not know the truth and is speaking a falsehood. (2:23). For you cannot know the Father apart from the Son, argues John. (2:23). The Son is the concrete, visible revelation of the Father's Being and character.

An Apostolic teaching to be Defended (2:24-27)

John admonishes the believers to stand firm in the confidence that what they believed in the beginning remain strong in them; that is, that Jesus is God's Son who entered into the world that they might have eternal life. To have the Son is simultaneously to have the Father who has promised eternal life through his Son. Do not diminish or alter this foundation truth: eternal life is in the Son. Stand secure in the face of opposition because the end of your faith is eternal fellowship with the Father and with his Son.

A Concluding Admonition (2:28-29)

As the teaching pastor of the community of believers, John wrote the first Epistle in which he confronts the false teaching that has arisen within the community. At the same time he admonishes the believers to stand firm in the faith which they have heard from the beginning. In admonishing them, he challenges them to "walk in the light as Jesus is in the light." (1:5). Stephen Smalley observes several conditions the believers need to embrace if they are to walk in the light as Jesus is in the light: (1) Renounce sin (1:8-2:2; 3:4-9)' (2)

Be obedient (2:3-11, 3:10-240; (3) Reject worldliness (2:12-17, 4:1-6); (4) Keep the Faith (2:18-29, 5:5-13). [47]

John, however, concludes in 2:28-29, with a word of encouragement and to create confidence that they may be sustained in their faith in the context of those who seek to deceive them and may be unashamed at the coming of Christ. (2: 26) The participle, "to deceive," writes Strecker, is a "conative present" that describes an attempted action not accomplished."[48] To encourage the believers John again takes up the concept of "anointing." (charisma). It is "you" (the "you" is given a personal and emphatic position), not the false teachers, who have the gift of charisma so that you have no need of anyone to teach you. (2:27). "The Spirit of truth, writes Strecker, being given to the community, leads them – like the Paraclete in the fourth Gospel – to acknowledge the truth."[49] It is "you" writes John, seeking to give confidence to the believers who are in possession of the "oil of anointing" that is identical with the possession of the Spirit and not the false teachers.

Section Two

The Gospel's Fundamental
Ethical Command "God is
Love"(I John 3: 1-5:13)

Lesson One: The Practices that Characterize the Walk of the Children of God(3:1-24)

Life in the family of God is characterized by various privileges and responsibilities, all of which are grounded and motivated by the biblical declaration: God is love.

Study Questions

When this section of the book has been read (3:1-24) and discussed, you should be able to:

(1) Explain the significance of the incarnation as the ultimate expression of God's love.

(2) Defend the command to love our brothers and sisters because of God's love for us.

(3) Understand and embrace the love and mercy of God that cancels our fear of divine judgment.

A Prospect to be cherished beyond all our aspirations (3:1-3)

When we are pressed down with uncertainty and doubt, we must cling to the truth that we "belong to God," and that God loves and cares for us. John states this truth clearly, "See what love the Father has given us, that we should be called the children of God" and concludes with the affirmative statement, "and that is what we are." (3:1a) With a different context but retaining the same truth, John writes in the Fourth Gospel, "To all who received him, to those who believed in his name, he gave the right to become the children of God – children born not of human descent, nor of natural descent, nor of human decision, nor a husband's will, but born of God." (John 1:12-13).

God's love overflows and calls the universe into existence on which God showers His goodness, not because of any necessity, but simply out of sheer love and grace. The incarnation and suffering love of Jesus Christ is God's primary self-revelation and self-communication, and therefore the archetype of all of God's activity toward us in redemption and creation. All of God's actions and deeds are guided and ground in the biblical declaration that God is love. T. F. Torrance put it this way, "God creates not out of necessity but purely in the freedom of love that God is; it is out of this intrinsic fellowship of personal being and love that God wills not to exist for the Divine Self alone and brings a world into existence, forms human beings out of the dust of the earth, and gives them an integrity of their own out of sheer grace and love so that God may share His communion of love and personal being with them. It is this incredible freedom of God's almighty power that reveals the astonishing character of God's activity that always seems to take us by surprise."[50] The incarnation, therefore, is intensely personal, for God himself came into the midst of our world of disorder and despair in order to preserve, heal, save, reconcile and redeem. If we ever doubt that God loves us, we need only to recall the incarnation. We are indeed the children of God and God has predestined for us an eternal reality beyond our most creative imaginations.

Adrio Konig expressed it this way, "The love of God is a love that goes out to a worthless object, giving it value. God does not love the world in the sense that he desires something that he does not have and can only get from humans. God's love for the world is a love that gives; a love that enriches the lives of humankind and only in this way enriches his own."[51] To assert that God is love is the deepest meaning of the doctrine of Christ's divinity and provides an insight into the core meaning of the doctrine of predestination as the ultimate expression and consummation of God's love for his children. The goal of predestination focuses, not first and foremost on the doctrine of salvation, but on the ultimate destiny of salvation; namely, the complete and final restoration of his children into that state for which God originally create us – conformed into the image of Christ.

A Problem to be Cleansed from all our Commitments (3:4-10)

The challenge that John presents in these verses is that believers are born of God and therefore do not sin. But such a declaration seems to contradict John's words in 2:1-2: "if anyone does sin, we have an "advocate with the Father, Jesus Christ, the Righteous One." So what does John mean by his words, "No one who is born of God will continue to sin, because God's seed remains him; he cannot go on sinning, because he has been born of God" (3:9) And then again, "No one who lives in him (God/ Christ) keeps on sinning; no one who continues to sin has either seen him or known him" (3:6).

In this specific section of verses (3:4-10), John is contrasting sin with injustice/justice (doing what is wrong) and, therefore, defines sin as lawlessness. (3:4, 7). Simultaneously, and without contradiction, John also identifies sin as the failure to love our brothers which is the essence of the law. (3:10) As Paul writes, "Love is the fulfillment of the law." (Rom. 13:10). If we are to embrace this teaching, we cannot, then, practice injustice and simultaneously have a confident relationship with God. For

John states, "Everyone who has this hope in him (that is, the hope and confidence of God's redeeming love) purifies (cleanses) himself, just as he is pure" (3:3). In other words, we cannot despise, mistreat, reject, and act unjustly or unlovingly toward our neighbor and claim to be walking in the light and love of Christ. As John clearly states, "Everyone who sins breaks the law; for sin is lawlessness (a failure to act justly, righteously or lovingly). (3: 10), As professor Strecker writes, "Committing sin is the opposite pole of practicing justice, which is acting righteously and was already spoken of in 2:29 and taken up again in 3:7 and 3:10. The point John is making, coupled with his choice of terms, express the concept that anyone who is guilty of sin is also guilty of lawlessness. In other words, John is teaching that whatever one considers sin to be in advance "the concept of lawlessness (anomia), as an overarching and summarizing expression, makes visible the fundamental structure of sin (hamartia); and therefore it can be equated with unrighteousness (adikia)."[52]

A Practice to be Consummated in all our Contacts (3:11-18)

John continues to exhort his followers to practice that which they have known from the beginning of their commitment to Christ; namely, to love their fellow believers. He emphasizes the importance of this command negatively by referring to the practice of Cain. By not mentioning Abel his exhortation stresses the negative side of his argument; namely, the opposition between love and injustice, good, and evil. Here again, John stresses that the practice of loving our brothers/sisters is a mark of belonging to Christ. He then draws the comparison, not simply between good and evil, but between failure to love and murder. The word translated as "murder" is also an expression for "killing." (The Septuagint translates the word as "murdering" or "slaughtering.")[53]

The practice of love entails self-sacrifice, forgiveness, and self-giving care while murder entails the opposite: the rejection of the hated person's very existence; that is, to treat the hated person as dead; hence the metaphor, "to murder." John, then, concludes by admonishing the believers not to give lip service to this fundamental command, but to practice love in daily conduct and in all circumstances. (3:18)

A Promise to be Claimed in all our fears. (3:19-24)

To practice love in all the circumstances of daily life is how we convince ourselves that we know the truth and can reassure our doubting hearts before God's day of judgment. Loving our brothers and sisters is how our hearts can be put at rest before the presence of God, if and when, our hearts should condemn us. In the Greek text the introductory verse 19, "by this" are explained by verse 20. The knowledge that the believers abide in the truth is based on believing that God is love and that this love is greater than the accusations of our hearts. From a different perspective, John is affirming the claim in 3:1 that we "belong to God" and this status is secured by the love God has for us. This conviction is furthermore ground in the teaching of verse 4:18; namely, that to practice love toward our brothers and sisters combined with the knowledge that God is love is of central importance for Christ-like conduct. To say that God knows everything is, writes Strecker, "simply another way of speaking of God's all-encompassing love."[54] The primary point in verse 20, then, expresses confidence that God's mercy and love will have the deciding word. To trust God's love toward us constitutes a cornerstone foundation for Christian living.

LESSON TWO: THE PRINCIPLES THAT CERTIFY THE WITNESS OF THE CHILDREN OF GOD (4:1-5:13)

This last division of the Epistle has its context in the fundamental affirmations that culminate in 5:6-13. The division is not clear cut. It appears, however, that it is the author's intention to lead up to a conclusion affirming the certainty of the faith, particularly at the moment when many were doubtful by the doctrinal disputes and the non-Christian conduct of some.

A Confession in the historical validity of Jesus Christ (4:1-6)

John returns to his primary concern; namely, the historical validity of Jesus as the Son of God. Strecker subdivides this section 4:1-6 this way. Verses 1-3 emphasize the need for discernment of different spirits. Verses 4-6 focus on "the relationship of the spirits to the world and the community set in opposition to false teaching within the framework of a God-world dualism."[55]

Critical to this section (4:1-6) is an understanding of the meaning of the word "spirit" or "spirits." The word "spirit' here refers to the guiding or directing source that motivates decision making and that expresses the personal dimensions of human existence. John assumes the existence of a variety of spirits, confirmed by the use of "every" (panti). For example, there are many spirits in the world, such as, the spirit of jealousy, of pride, of arrogance, of lust, of joy, of compassion, etc. Robert C. Roberts rightly points out that humans, in contrast with non-human creatures, live by adopted conceptions of what our life is and ought to be. We impose order on ourselves and our world by the way we picture them. . . . Each spirit or spirituality is a different "conception" of what human life is and ought to be and is controlled and shaped by a different set of leading concepts. Each involves, for the person who has imbibed a particular spirituality or spirit, a differing set of emotional responses, of judgments about what is appropriate, and of characteristic virtues and vices."[56] For this reason, warns Roberts, "Christians ought to be distressed when attempts are made to mix the Christian picture of self and world with the pictures which govern other spiritualities or spirits.[57] John of course, intends the reference "spirits" to apply to the teaching of the false teachers. He admonishes the believers, therefore, "not to believe" every spirit. The verb, believe, in 4:1 could also be translated as "trust." Trust seems to carry a preferred meaning for the false teaching is described as constituting "lies" that are from the Devil and not from God (2:21) and are intended to "deceive" (2:26) or "lead astray." (3:7). John, therefore, describes the "spirit" of the false teachings as the "spirit of error" (4:6).

On the other hand, however, the believers possess "the" Spirit and therefore can discern the "truth" (3:28). The false "spirits" speak from the viewpoint of the world and therefore the world listens to them. (4:4-5). Believers, however, are born of the Spirit of God which is also the "Spirit of Truth." For this reason the people of the spirits of the world do not listen to them. "The false teachings John's community is encountering," contends Strecker," is not an isolated phenomenon and cannot be limited to a particular historical period. They are an enduring and pervasive danger that constantly accompanies the Christian community on its journey through the ages."[58]

In verses 4-6 John develops the basic thesis that "the criterion that aids discernment of spirits is the apostolic confession; (4:2) namely, that God has come in flesh in the person of Jesus Christ. John develops this criterion by making a positive statement (you are from God) followed by a negative counterpart (they are from the world). The false teachers speak and listen to the spirit of falsehood in the world; but you speak and listen to the Spirit of truth. (4:5-6). Do not allow the spirit of this age to alter or diminish the basic core of the faith-confession; namely, that in Jesus Christ we have not only forgiveness of sin, restored fellowship with God, but also the prospect of a completely renewed world, including human existence.

A Commandment of Practical Value (4:7-5:5)

John again returns to a practical concern; namely, the critical importance of the practice of love. Love is the dominant characteristic or evidence that one knows God. The opposite is, therefore, also true: The person who does not practice agape love does not know God. Strecker clarifies when he writes, "The sphere of agape is not a magical phenomenon. Instead, so far as it includes human beings, it presupposes that human actions are marked by accountability . . . Christians who make love a reality recognize or acknowledge God by that very act (2:13-14; cf. 5:20).[59] The world, on the other hand, demonstrates its denial of God by its opposite; namely, injustice, anger, and lawlessness. (3:1-6). But what is John's meaning of "love." Agape love does not arise from within the initiative of the human heart. Rather it comes from the heart of God in the self-giving and self-sacrificing act of God in the incarnation for the sake of sinners. (4:10). The incarnation is a window into the heart of God's loving essence.

Elmer M. Colyer expressed the thought of T.F. Torrance on God's love this way, "Only because of God's self-revelation in Jesus Christ ... do we come to know and understand something of this love of God that surpasses knowledge."[60] If we should ever doubt the love of God for us, we need only to reflect on the incarnation. God, the almighty creator of heaven and earth whose rational existence declares the greatness of God and a love that produced them, entered into human existence as Jesus Christ, suffered at the hands of his creatures, beaten, humiliated, and experienced the shame of death in order that sinful, rebellious humanity might find freedom from its sinful captivity and experience communion with the love and person of God. T. F. Torrance writes, "It is a love that flows between the Father, the Son, and the Spirit; it freely flows in an outward movement of loving activity toward us with whom God creates a communion of love corresponding to the Communion of Love which he ever is in himself."[61]

Within his emphasis on the significance of divine love, John points to love's practical function in relation to God. John writes, "There is no fear in love. But perfect love drives out fear, because fear has to do with punishment. The one who fears is not made perfect in love." (4: 18). John returns to the theme of 3:21-22. Here, however, he offers a clear word of encouragement when our conscience condemns us. John writes, "God is love. Whoever lives in love lives in God and God in him." (4:16b-17). Strecker again clarifies and guides our understanding when he writes, "The author did not intend to say that God, as a 'kind of human fellowship" is simply an object for theological anthropology and ethics. Instead, Christian ethical actions presuppose the reality of God's agape love."[62] Divine love is all-embracing and is bestowed on human beings out of divine grace. However, we must be careful here: Two things are not inter-changeable; that is. To assert that love is God is not to assert that God is love simply related to itself. What is important for John is that God has appeared as one who loves. In other words, God's love is not simply an abstract concept, but "has accommodated itself to the human capacity to experience it."[63]

Divine love gives value and worth to that which is in itself unworthy. Such divine love overcame the world in the sending of Jesus Christ to die for the sins of the world. The person who loves God also embraces God's loving commandments because the person who loves God also trusts in the goodness of God's commands. Obedience, therefore, is essentially an act of trust in God's guiding commands. The foundation for this trust resides in the belief that God has come into the world to redeem us from evil and sin's destructive ways. John, therefore, writes, "Who is it that overcomes the world? Only he who believes (trusts) that Jesus is the Son of God." (5:5)

A Conclusion of Theological Significance (5:1-5)

John returns to his basic theological and ethical theses: the incarnation as the supreme example of God's love and the command to love one another. The believer who obeys God's commands abides in God's love because he trusts in the loving-goodness of God's directing commands. The importance of the confession that Jesus is indeed God come in the flesh is an essential dimension of the Christian faith. Again professor Strecker conveys John's meaning with summarial clarity, "The Son is 'unique' because only in him is God's agape love manifest; only he represents the "glory of God" to the world (John 1:14) and reveals to humanity an offer of life that it cannot accomplish (or find) in and of itself."[64]

Eternal Life and the Tragedy of Sin (5: 6-12)

John concludes the Epistle by confirming and encouraging the community of believers with the truth emphasized throughout the Epistle.

(1) That through the confessional belief that Jesus Christ is God come in the flesh they have eternal life. (5:11-12). "I write these things to you who believe in the name of the Son of God: so that you may know that you have eternal life." (5: 13).

(2) That this confessional belief is the basis for their confidence before the judgment seat of God.

(3) That they are the children and object of God's love. This divine love assures them that God hears whatever they ask of him.

(4) That forgiveness is available for them if they should fall short of God's standards as his children.

John now turns attention to the possibility of sin within the community and how they should respond. John writes, "If anyone sees his brother commit a sin that does not lead to death, he should pray and God will give him life; that is, forgiveness. I refer to those whose sin does not lead to death. There is, however, a sin that leads to death. I am not saying that he should pray about that. All wrong doing is sin, and there is a sin that leads to death." (5: 16-17). John's statements are straight-forward and not a little perplexing in view of the nature of Christian love and Christ as our "advocate" in the face of sin coupled with the teaching that Christ is the "sacrifice of atonement" for our sins before God. The focus of John in verses 16-17 may have their background in verses 13-15. The section begins with the author's intention to stress the certainty of eternal life among the members of the community.

The confidence that they have eternal life leads John to offer pastoral advice that they pray for their brothers/sisters. The perplexing verses in 5:16-17 continue the emphasis on caring for fellow believers within the community coupled with an admonition that in some particular cases of sin, prayer is not his focus. J.B. Phillip's paraphrase of verse 16-17 is helpful here. Phillips writes, "If any of you should see his brother committing a sin (I don't mean deliberately turning his back on God and embracing evil) he should pray to God for him and secure fresh life for the sinner. It is possible to commit sin that is a deliberate embracing of evil and that leads to spiritual death – that is not the sort of sin I have in mind when I recommend prayer for the sinner."[65]

The two phrases, *"sin that leads to death"* and *"sin not leading to death"* are critical to any interpretation of John's exhortation to love and care for one another. Smalley proposes that a possible or "likely background to the notion of sin leading, or not leading to death is to found in the distinction drawn in the OT and Judaism, between inadvertent and deliberate sins. Sacrifice and prayer is effective for unconscious sins; but willful or deliberate sins could only be removed by the death of the sinner."[66] Smalley, therefore, concludes "The likelihood that the fundamental (background) of the Johannine circle was Jewish-Christian strengthens this possibility."[67]

If a Jewish-Christian background is accepted, the practice of the early Church becomes helpful. The early believers held the view that any believer who committed apostasy under persecution and pressure of death could not be forgiven. In the case of unintentional sins within the community, prayer is to be offered with the confidence that God hears. Num.18:22 appears to support this interpretation; namely, that the notion of an unforgiveable sin results in physical death. It seems, however, that John transforms the Old Testament admonition in terms of spiritual death. The author to the Epistle to the Hebrews conveys similar, or perhaps the same notion, when he writes, "It is impossible for those who have once been enlightened, who have tasted the heavenly gift, who have shared in the Holy Spirit, who have tasted the goodness of the word of God and the powers of the coming age, if they fall away, to be brought back to repentance, because to their loss they are crucifying the Son of God all over again, and subjecting him to public disgrace." (Heb. 6:4-6).

This so-called "second repentance," due to apostasy, closes the door to the eschatological hope of eternal life. Even though the precise offense is not stated in I John Strecker's comment is insightful here, "though a strict casuistry (the practice of struggling with unclear cases of right and wrong) is still foreign to the time of the writing of First John, this idea of "mortal sin" has its place in the dualistic and eschatological context of this homily and is to be understood as the radical opposite to the highest good of salvation, eternal life." Given John's consistent emphasis on the forgiveness of sin (2:1) and as long as a person continues to reject Jesus as the Son of God, this attitude of rejection bars the door to salvation since it rejects the very means by which eternal salvation may be granted to the sinner. John seems to have in mind the false teachers who clearly make this claim and by inference are living under the judgment of God.

The Certainty of Divine Witness: A Confirmation for their Faith (5: 6-20)

John again admonishes the children of God to keep the faith; namely, that through belief in Jesus Christ as the Son of God, they have forgiveness of sin and eternal life. This confession constitutes a foundational belief of the Christian faith. In support John, then, offers divine confirmation of this confessional belief in verses 6-8. John writes, "This is the one who came by water and blood – Jesus Christ. He did not come by water only, but by water and blood. And it is the Spirit who testifies because the Spirit is the truth. For there are three that testify: the Spirit, the water, and the blood and the three are in agreement." (5:6-8).

These particular verses have been variously interpreted. Some, for example, interpret these verse from a sacramental viewpoint' that is, as referring to the communion table or to the Eucharist. Others, however, have rejected these verses as being in the original text. Nevertheless, the verses seem to fit nicely within the flow of John's argument to give confirmation both to the exhortation to keep the faith but also to offer a solid ground for their belief in Jesus as the Son of God.

The point John is making in verses 6-8 is to provide an authoritative witness underlying the community's commitment of faith. While a sacramental interpretation can be imposed on these verses, it seems unlikely that John is using the terms "water" and "blood" (verse v: 6) to refer to the communion table or the Eucharist. While a sacramental interpretation goes back to Luther and Calvin, it involves difficulties. Stephen S. Smalley notes that the two nouns water and blood should be taken in the contextual sense of John's central argument.[68] In other words, the statement in verse six, ("not in water only") "makes it clear that a meaning must be found for these terms which allows them to be distinguished; whereas the sacraments of baptism and the Lord's Supper manifestly complement each other."[69] John's central argument in the Epistle centers on the historical presence of Christ and his incarnate life on earth, not with his continuing manifestation in the sacramental life of the Church.

To fortify his point John notes the place of human testimony that is accepted within human society. Without trust in the testimony of others, the world could not maintain order or civil judgments (truth-decisions). (5:9). Recognizing the accepted role of human testimony in making just (legal) judgments, John presents a superior testimony; namely, that of the three: water, blood, and Spirit. These three constitute the testimony of God and are, therefore, worthy of greater trust and assurance underlying their faith-commitment. Strecker writes, "The testimony of the three is the testimony of God. It is superior to all human affirmations, even when these latter are supported by the testimony of many witnesses"[70] (5:8) and therefore provide a greater assurance (or confirmation) against those teachers who claim a special spiritual authority.[71]

Given the context and concern of John with the historical revelation of God in Jesus Christ, it appears more likely that John is stressing the confirmation of Jesus' earthly life from beginning to end which reveals Jesus as the "Son of God" and the "Savior" of the world. Hence, Jesus' baptism marks God's own seal of approval on Jesus' coming ministry as the "Savior" of the world ("You are my Son whom I love, with you I am well pleased '(Luke 3: 21-22). The Spirit, then, like a dove, came upon Jesus in order to empower him for his coming ministry. The blood refers to the completion of Jesus' ministry on the cross; that is, to the consummation of the Jesus' earth mission.

Water or baptism then simply denotes his separation or consecration to a specific ministry and Spirit his anointing and empowerment for that mission. The "blood" then refers to the consummation of Christ's earthly ministry on the cross that verifies Christ's deity with the resurrection from the dead. (Rom. 1:1-4-5). In a word, John offers a divine confirmation to the believers' commitment to Jesus as the sole "Savior" of the world.

Summary of First John

John stresses two important truths in his First Epistle. (1) The revelation of God's being as "light" refers to the historical disclosure of God's person and redemptive work in Jesus Christ. This concrete revelation is stated straight forwardly at the outset of the Epistle. Note the empirical terms (hearing, seeing, touching, and experiencing) used by John to confirm the historical revelation of God in Jesus Christ. John writes, "That which was from the beginning, which we have heard, which we have seen with our eyes, which we have looked at and our hands have touched- this we proclaim concerning the Word of Life. The life appeared; we have seen it and testify to it, and we proclaim to you the eternal life, which was with the Father and has appeared to us" (1:1-2. This gift of eternal life comes only through Jesus Christ. John, therefore, concludes his Epistle with the words, "We know also that the Son of God has come and has given us understanding, so that we may know him (God) who is true. And we are in him who is true – even in his Son Jesus Christ. He (Jesus) is the true God and eternal life." (5:20)

The second truth is that God is love. Here John stresses the incarnation of Jesus Christ as the supreme example of God's love with the admonition that believers need to express this love toward one another. (4:9-12).

Endnotes

1. I am using the terms community, church, and Johannine circle synonymously.

2. Marla J. Selvidge, Exploring the New Testament, 2nd ed. (New Jersey: Uppe Saddle River/Prentice Hall, 2003). P. 339.

3. Georg Strecker The Johannine Letters, Trans. By Linda M. Maloney and ed., by Harold Attridge, (Minneapolis: Fortress Press).p. xxxv.

4. Ibid., p. xxxv.

5. Stephen S. Smalley, Word Biblical Commentary, 1, 2, 3, John, (FWaco: Word Publishers, 1984). P. xxxii

6. Eusebius Historia Eccl. 3.39.c3-4. The History of the Church from Chris to Constantine, trans and with an introduction by G. A. Williamson (Harmondsworth: Penguin, 1955), 3.39. c3-4.

7. Marla J. Selvidge, Ibid., p. 345.

8. David Barr, The New Testament Story, An Introduction, 3rd ed., (Watsworth Group/Thomson Learning Inc. 2002). P. 411.

9. Corp. herm, p.13.3

10. Paul S. Rees, The Adequate man: paul in Philippians, (Revell Co., 1959). p22.

11. N.T. Wright,Evil and the Justice of God, (Downers Grove: InterVarsity Press, 2006) p.77.

12. Ibid., p. 18.

13. Robert. S. Brumbaugh, The Philosophers of Greece, (London: George Allen & Unwin Lt.,1966).

14. Ray S. Anderson, On Being Human, (Grand Rapids, Eerdmans,1982) pp. 21-23.

15. Frederick R. Tennant, The Source of the Doctrine of the Fall and Original Sin, Reprint (University of Cambridge, 1902), and Fredrick Schleiermacher, The Christian Faith, ed. H.R. Mackintosh and J. S. Stewart, 2nd, ed. (Philadelphia: Fortress, 1928).

16. John Smith, Reason and God: Encounters of Philosophy with Religion, (New Haven: Yale University Press,

17. John Claypool, This Incomplete One: Words Occasioned by the Death of a Young Person, Michael D. Bush, ed. (Grand Rapids: Wm. B. Eerdmans, 2006). P.38

18. Ibid., (Quoted by Claypool) p. 38.

19. Ibid., p. 39.

20. Ibid, p.41.

21. Ibid, p. 44-45.

22. Ibid, p 42.

23. Ibid, p 64.

24. Ibid, p. 64.

25.   David Bartlett, "Erick Hansen," in This Incomplete One, Op. Cit., p. 26.

26.   Ben Witterington III, Revelation, The Cambridge Bible Commentary, (New York: Cambridge University Press, 2003). P. 257.

27.   Georg Strecker, The Johannine Letters, Hermeneia – A critical and historical commentary on the Bible, 1996). P.28.

28.   Rudolf Schnackenbury, The Epistles, "Wahrhei in Glaubenssazennach dem erssen Johannessbbrief,"Karl Rahner, ed., Zum Problem Unfehlbarkeit, (Freiburg: Herder), 1971

29.   George Hendry, The Holy Spirlt in Christian Theology, (Westminster Press, 1965). p. 26.

30.   H. Q. Hamilton, The Holy Spirit and Eschatology in Paul, SJT Occasional Papers. No. 6, (Edinburgh: Oliver & Boyd, 1957) p. 6.

31.   Strecker, Ibid, p. 30.

32.   Smalley, Op. Cit.,p 43.

33.   Strecker, Op. Cit., p. 40

34.   Ibid, p.41

35.   Ibid, p.41.

36.   Ibid, p.41.

37.   A Greek-English Lexicon of the New Testament and other Early Christian Literature (BDAG) 3ed., (Chicago: University of Chicago Press, 2000). P 996.

38.   Strecker, Op. Cit., p.58-59.

39.   Smalley, Ibid, p.81.

40.   Strecker, Ibid., p.59.

41. Ibid., p. 63; Polycarp. Phil. L7:1.

42. Anthony Hoekema, The Bible and the future, (Grand Rapids: Eerdmans, 1979) p.137.

43. Strecker, Op. Cit., p. 63.

44. Ibid., pp. 236-237.

45. Ibid, p. 68.

46. Ibid, p. 44

47. Stephen S. Smalley, Op. cit., pp. 27-138. (See; Table of Contents)

48. Strecker,, Op. Cit., p.76.

49. Ibid, p. 76

50. Elmer C. Colyer, How To Read T.F. Torrance, (Downers Grove: InterVarsity Press, 2001). P. 161; T.F. Torrance, The Christian Doctrine of God, (Edinburgh: T & T. Clark, 1996). P. 140.

51. Adrio Konig, Here Am I; A Believer's Reflection on God, (Mashall, Moran & Scott, 1982). P. 37.

52. Georg Strecker, Op. Cit., p. 94.

53. Ibid., p. 109.

54. Ibid., p. 123.

55. Strecker, Ibid., p. 131.

56. Robert C. Roberts, "What is Spirituality?" The Reformed Journal, August, 193) p. 14.

57. Ibid, p 14.

58. Strecker, Op. Cit., p. 133.

59.   Ibid., p. 144

60.   Elmer C. Colyer, Op. Cit., 146.

61.   Ibid., p. 166. See also: T.T. Torrance, Mediation, (Colorado Springs: Helmers & Howard Publishers (New Edition, 1992; originally published, 1983) p. 109.

62.   Strecker,Op. Cit., p. 148

63.   Ibid., p. 149.

64.   Ibid, p. 151.

65.   J. B. Philips, The New Testament in Modern English, (London: Geoffrey Bles, 1960) p. 507.

66.   Smalley, Op. Cit., p. 297.

67.   Ibid., p. 298.

68.   Strecker, Op. Cit., p. 203.

69.   Smalley, Op. Cit., 277.

70.   Ibid., p. 277.

71.   Strecker, p.192-193